# UNCLE LEO'S ADVENTURES
## in the
## Siberian Jungle

**Yannets Levi** has written books and for television. Born in Israel to a family of storytellers, he remembers being surrounded by stories ever since he was a kid, told by his parents, uncles and aunts.

His Uncle Leo's Adventures series is one of Israel's most popular children's book series and has sold more than 450,000 copies in Israel alone. The series has also been published in the Czech Republic, South Korea and Japan. He has also written another children's book, *Mrs Rosebud is No Monster*, and two books for adults.

**Yaniv Shimony** is a graduate of the Bezalel Academy of Art and Design in Jerusalem, considered the top art school in Israel. After completing his studies, he worked as Art Director in some of Israel's largest advertising agencies. Currently, his work focuses on illustrating children's books. In 2008, Shimony won an award for Children's Book Illustration from the Israel Museum for his work in *Uncle Leo's Adventures in the Romanian Steppes*.

Other Books in the Series:

*Uncle Leo's Adventures in the Romanian Steppes*
*Uncle Leo's Adventures in the Swiss Desert*
*Uncle Leo's Adventures in the West Pole*

# UNCLE LEO'S ADVENTURES

in the
## Siberian Jungle

## Yannets Levi

Illustrated by Yaniv Shimony
Translated by Margo Eyon

RED TURTLE
RUPA

Published in Red Turtle by
Rupa Publications India Pvt. Ltd 2014
7/16, Ansari Road, Daryaganj
New Delhi 110002

*Sales centres:*
Allahabad Bengaluru Chennai
Hyderabad Jaipur Kathmandu
Kolkata Mumbai

First published in Hebrew in 2009
This edition copyright © Yannets Levi 2014
Illustration copyright © Yaniv Shimony 2007
Translated by Margo Eyon

ISBN: 978-81-291-3464-6

First impression 2014

10 9 8 7 6 5 4 3 2 1

The moral right of the author has been asserted.

This edition is for sale in the Indian subcontinent only.

# Contents

# Introduction

My big brother thinks he's the smartest kid in the world. Well, maybe not the smartest, but smarter than me, even though he's only two years older than I am. He's definitely taller, that's for sure, and faster, and maybe even stronger. But that doesn't mean he's smarter. And it doesn't give him the right to make fun of me. But he always makes fun of me! When I laugh about something, he laughs at me. When I cry about something, he laughs at me as well.

When he has friends over and they start whispering and I ask, 'What? What are you talking about?', he laughs and says, 'You'll understand when you're older.'

How I hate that line! How much could I grow, and what more could I understand in just two more years, when I'm my brother's age? And even then, he'll still be bigger than me and he'll still be able to tell me, 'You'll understand when you're older.'

Mom told me that her big sister used that line on her too. 'You'll see,' Mom said. 'He'll stop eventually. Don't let it get to you.' But it *does* get to me.

Ever so often, Dad tries to help by telling Graham, 'Be a friend to your little brother.' But it doesn't do any good. My brother doesn't listen.

I told Uncle Leo about it and he said, 'I say, "You'll understand when you're smaller."'

'What do you mean?' I asked.

'The smaller the better,' he answered. And if Uncle Leo says so, it must be true, because Uncle Leo has had crazy adventures all over the world and knows lots of stuff.

Uncle Leo comes to visit us every Wednesday. Uncle Leo isn't just an ordinary uncle. Mom says, 'Uncle Leo is a great bargain. You don't find an uncle like that every day.'

On Wednesdays, while my brother plays with his friends and thinks he's the smartest guy in the world, Uncle Leo and I sit on the balcony. Uncle Leo tells me about all the adventures he has had. And now I'm going to tell you these stories. I swear that everything I tell you is true. I didn't make any of it up. I heard it all with my very own ears, straight from Uncle Leo.

By the way, my name is Andy. My father's name is Eliot, my mother's is Daphne, my brother's is Graham, and my Uncle Leo's—as you might have guessed—is Uncle Leo!

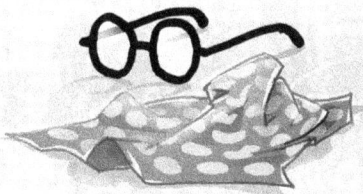

# Uncle Leo Digs a Tunnel

One Wednesday, I went into my brother's room. Before I could even say a word, Graham snapped at me. 'Didn't you see the sign on the door?' he said.

'What sign?'

'That sign,' he said, pointing. 'It says right here—"No Strangers Allowed!" Can't you read?'

'Of course I can read,' I said, 'but since when are strangers not allowed into your room?'

'Since right now,' said Graham. 'Get out!'

'But you *know* me,' I said. 'I'm not a stranger.'

'You're a stranger because I say you're a stranger,' said Graham. Then he shoved me and shouted, 'Now get out!'

I had wanted to ask Graham to play checkers, but I

1

had no choice but to leave his room.

Uncle Leo, who had just come to visit, appeared outside Graham's door.

'How are you?' he asked.

'All right,' I said in a voice that probably didn't sound very all right.

'"No Strangers Allowed"?' Uncle Leo asked, reading what was written on Graham's door.

'That's the new rule,' I explained.

'Just like in Decria,' said Uncle Leo.

'Decria?' I asked. 'Where's that?'

'It's a special city in the Siberian jungle,' said Uncle Leo.

We went to the balcony and sat down.

'What's so special about this Decria?' I asked.

So Uncle Leo told me.

'Once, on one of my trips to the Siberian jungle, I happened upon the fortified city of Decria. As soon as I entered the city gates, I noticed something was odd: everyone was walking around in their underwear. It was a really cold day, freezing cold, in fact. Everything was covered in snow. But everyone was just wearing underwear. All the children, all the women, all the men— they all wore only underpants and undershirts. People were shivering with cold and sneezing all over the place. Some people were huddling together to keep warm. Others were jumping up and down to heat themselves up. People's teeth were rattling so loudly that you could hear them from far away. Many people just kept blowing their noses, over and over again.

'I went up to a man in the marketplace and asked, "Why is everyone walking around in their underwear?"

'"I-i-it's the n-n-new dec-c-cree by our qu-qu-queen, Decrioly the One and Only. She ru-ru-ru-ruled that today, everyone must go wi-wi-wi-without clo-o-o-othes!" The man shivered and sneezed, "Achoo, achee!"

'That night, before I fell asleep, I thought, *What a strange kingdom! And what a strange decree!* But I didn't know that in the morning, an even bigger surprise would be waiting for me.'

'What happened in the morning?' I asked Uncle Leo.

'When I got up the next morning and looked out the window, I was happy to see that the people of Decria had gone back to wearing clothes. But I soon discovered an even greater hullabaloo. Everyone was fully dressed, yes, but they kept bumping into each other. Some people were tripping over boxes and falling into ditches along the side

of the road. Others were bumping into poles and crashing into walls. Children were calling for their mothers, fathers were calling for their children, but almost no one was able to find what they wanted. When I went outside, I found out why: everyone had their eyes closed!

'I walked to the marketplace and approached a woman standing next to a watermelon stand with her eyes closed. "Excuse me, ma'am!" I said.

'"Who's that? Who's calling me? Where are you?" she asked. Of course, she couldn't see me.

'"My name is Uncle Leo," I told her. "I'm right here. Next to you. On your right."

'The woman tried to turn her face towards me, but since her eyes were closed she couldn't do it.

'"Why does everyone have their eyes closed today?" I asked.

'"Oh," said the woman, "that's the new decree by our queen, Decrioly the One and Only. She ruled that today, everyone must do everything with their eyes closed. We must walk with our eyes closed, eat with our eyes closed, and work with our eyes closed!"

'"Why?" I asked. "What's the reason for this decree?"

'"That's just the way it is in Decria," said the woman.

"Every day, Queen Decrioly the One and Only announces a new decree for the day."

'The woman walked right up to me and felt my head with her hands. I didn't understand why she was doing that. "Tell me," she said. "Does this watermelon look good to you?"

"'That's not a watermelon!" I told her. "That's my head!"

"'Oh," said the woman. "Sorry. I thought your head was a watermelon." Then she tried felt her way and stumbled off.

'That's how the days passed in Decria. The queen's heralds came to the city square every morning and proclaimed the day's new decree. One day, the people of Decria were ordered to sleep by day and work at night. That was a tiring decree. The next day, they weren't allowed to drink anything—not even water. Needless to say, that was a very dry decree. One day, they could only talk by shouting. By nightfall, all the people were hoarse. Another day, they had to cackle like chickens instead of talking. That decree was kind of funny, actually.'

'And what happened to people who didn't obey the decrees?' I asked.

Uncle Leo looked at me with a worried face. 'Whoever

didn't follow the decrees,' he said, 'received a heavy punishment. Police officers were dispatched throughout the kingdom. Anyone caught violating a decree was taken to the palace and executed!'

'*Executed?*' I was shocked.

'Yes. Life in Decria was very tough. Luckily, foreigners weren't required to comply with the decrees, so I didn't have to follow the rules. Queen Decrioly's police officers didn't take me to the palace. But, one day, everything changed,' said Uncle Leo, lowering his eyes. 'Everything changed, Andy,' he repeated.

'What changed?' I asked. 'What happened?'

'One day, the heralds came to the city square and announced:

> "*Decrioly the One and Only, our fair queen,*
> *today issued a new decree, smart and keen:*
> *All strangers in our magnificent city*
> *Will be captured with no exception or pity.*
> *Henceforth they'll be treated like rubbish and soot*
> *And put to death under an elephant's foot.*"

'The heralds put up signs in the streets which said:

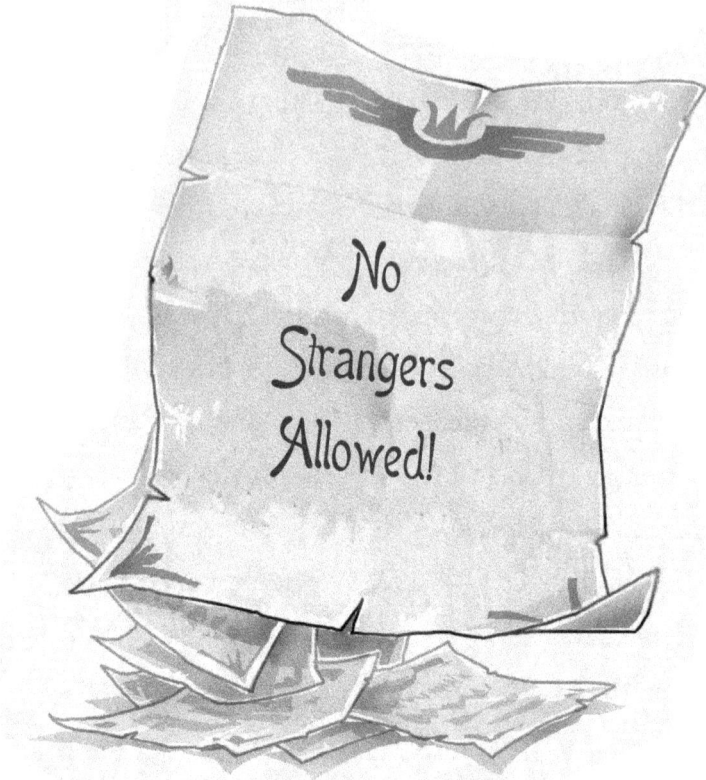

"No Strangers Allowed!" I heard the decree, read the signs, and got really scared! I myself was a stranger, a foreigner, in Decria! I hadn't been born there! And if the police caught me, I'd be in serious trouble!

'Immediately, I decided to run away. I set out at once, but had only gone two steps before a couple of police officers clamped their hands down on my shoulders.

"'You!" they yelled in unison.

"'What's your name?" asked the tall officer.

"'And how are you called?" shouted the fat officer.

"'I'm Uncle Leo," I answered, trembling.

"'Were you born in Decria?" asked the tall officer.

"'And are you a native of our kingdom?" asked the fat officer.

"'No, I wasn't born in Decria," I said.

"'Then we are taking you to the palace," said the tall officer.

"'You are coming with us to the queen's court," ordered the fat officer.

"'Queen Decrioly will deal with you," announced the tall one.

"'Decrioly the One and Only!" added the fat one.'

Uncle Leo, sitting with me on the balcony, fell silent. He took a deep breath and exhaled slowly through his nostrils.

'Uncle Leo,' I said, worried. 'What happened at the palace? What did the queen do to you?'

Uncle Leo continued. 'I reached the palace with the two police officers. They took me to Queen Decrioly.

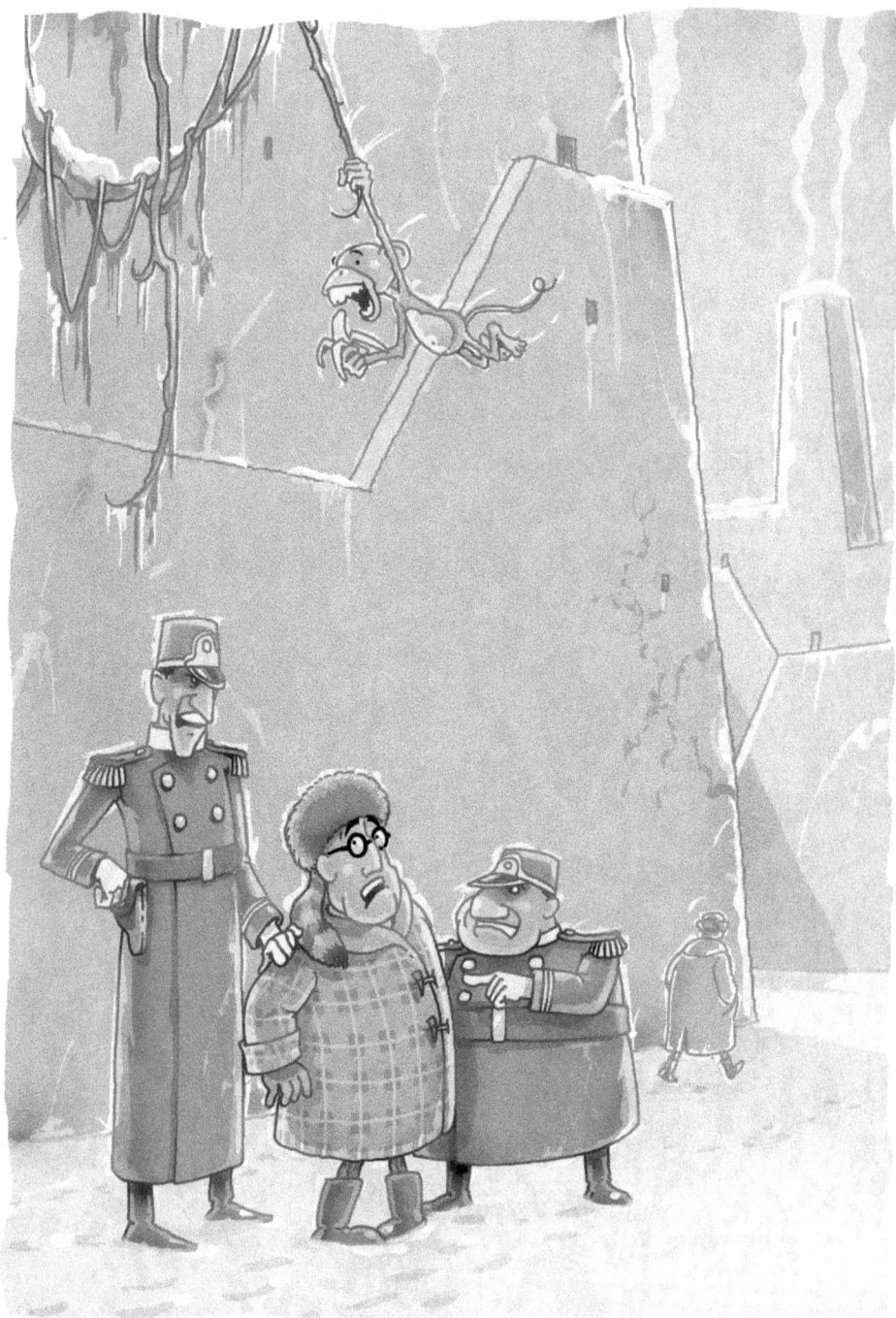

"'We found a stranger,' they told her.

"'Well, well!' said the queen. "I was getting anxious. I must have an execution before lunch. It's the best appetizer!" Then Queen Decrioly lifted her sceptre, and with no further ado said, "If within the next ten seconds you make me an offer that no one has ever come up with before, then your life will be spared. If not, you'll be meeting our elephant's foot!"

'No sooner had she finished speaking than she started counting, "One, two, three…" Quickly, I tried to think of an amazing offer. I said, "I'll make you a quiche with five different kinds of onions."

"'…four…I've already had quiches made with eight kinds!" said the queen, and kept on counting.

"'I'll carry you piggyback throughout the palace!'"

"'…five…I already have a special servant for that,' said the queen as she resumed counting.

"'…seven, eight…'"

"'Hey!' I shouted. "Six comes after five. What about six?"

"'You have another second and a half!' said the queen. "Bring in the elephant!" she commanded and continued counting.

An enormous, terrifying elephant entered the room and came towards me.

'I thought and thought and thought, but couldn't come up with any idea! Then, in the last half-second, I uttered these words: "I'll dig a tunnel to the other side of the earth and tell you what's over there!"

'Queen Decrioly stopped counting. "How disappointing," she said. "Very disappointing indeed. I didn't think you'd be able to offer me anything special, but your idea is truly surprising. Give him a shovel!" she ordered. A servant came over and handed me a shovel. The two police officers escorted me to a field outside the gates of the kingdom.

'*What am I doing? I thought. Why did I make such an impossible offer to the queen? How can I dig a tunnel to the other side of the world? From here to there is more than 12,000 kilometers! That's really*, really *far!*

'I didn't know what to do. I stood in the field. The two police officers looked at me. I had no choice. I had to start digging.'

'But Uncle Leo,' I said. 'You couldn't possibly have dug to the other side of the earth!'

'Of course not,' said Uncle Leo. 'That would have been

impossible! I dug and dug and dug deep down into the ground, but obviously I wasn't going to reach the other side of the earth any time soon. As I was digging, though, an idea came to my mind. I changed the direction of my digging and started digging a tunnel under the kingdom. Eventually, I reached the other side of the wall that surrounded it.'

'And then you escaped?' I asked Uncle Leo.

'No,' he replied. 'When I got to the other side of the wall, I rested for a few days. Then I went back through the tunnel and up to the police officers who were waiting for me outside at the other end.

'I told them, "That's it, I've returned from the other side of the earth." They immediately took me back to Queen Decrioly.

"'Queen Decrioly," I began.

"'The One and Only," added the queen.

"'Certainly," I said. "I dug a tunnel and reached the other side of the earth. If you wish, I will tell you what that's like."

"'Tell me right away!" ordered the queen.

"'On the other side of the earth there is a city."

"'A city?"

"'An absolutely ordinary city," I said. "It has some good

people, and some people who are not so good. It has some loyal citizens and some citizens who are not so loyal. There are some nice people and some less-than-nice people."

"'That sounds like a very boring city,' said the queen.

"'On the contrary,' I said. "It's actually a very interesting city, because it has a very special queen."

"'A special queen?' asked Queen Decrioly. "How is she special?"

"'The queen almost never leaves the palace. She doesn't know the people in her own city. She doesn't know how they live. She doesn't know that they are nice. She only knows how to issue decrees upon them. Terrible decrees."

"'Why does she do such a thing? Why does she make decrees?"

"'It's hard to say…no one has ever managed to get an answer from her, because one of the decrees is that she must never be asked any questions."

"'What kind of a queen is this? I myself make decrees so that the people will not forget me, but this queen sounds really stupid. What pointless cruelty! What senseless decrees!"

"'The city is marvellous, but the queen is…difficult," I continued. "It was a fascinating visit indeed. And if you want, I'll take you there," I offered.

'"To that city? Isn't it dangerous?"

'"For a queen like you? They'll give you a majestic welcome."

'The queen descended from her throne and said, "Come. Let's go immediately."

'The queen and I left in a grand procession, and went to where I had dug the tunnel. The royal guards waited outside, and Queen Decrioly and I entered the tunnel. We crawled into the earth and emerged on the other side of the tunnel, right next to the back entrance of the fortified city of Decria.

'Queen Decrioly didn't recognize the back entrance, since she seldom left the palace. We entered the city, Queen Decrioly's city. But Queen Decrioly didn't even know that she was visiting Decria, as she had almost never visited the city streets.

'As soon as we stepped foot in the city, the citizens recognized the queen and bowed low.

'"Wow," said Queen Decrioly. "The people here show great respect to visitors."

'"I told you, the people in this city are very nice," I said.

'The citizens of Decria were astonished to see their queen walking freely in the streets.

"'How lovely that you came to visit us," said one woman.

"'We never believed the day would come when you would come down to see us," said another man.

'The people of the city treated her with respect and awe. They offered her food and drink. They made way for her and invited her to their homes.

"'I have never visited such a wonderful place. Why does their queen abuse them so?" Queen Decrioly asked me. But then she noticed a sign saying: "No Strangers Allowed!" The decree was written underneath.

"'My goodness," said Queen Decrioly in a panic. "Look at what that says! They don't want strangers here. All foreigners will be taken to the queen's palace and put to death under an elephant's foot! We must escape at once!"

'Queen Decrioly began hurrying back the way we had come. The people of Decria watched in bewilderment. She skipped and jumped, rushed and ran, and suddenly saw two police officers ahead of her. "My, oh my! They're going to catch us!" she cried. "*Ee ee ee!*" she shrieked in terror, panting and jumping up and down on the spot.

'The people were confounded. They wondered what had happened to their Queen. They went up to her and said, "Our One and Only Queen, why are you so

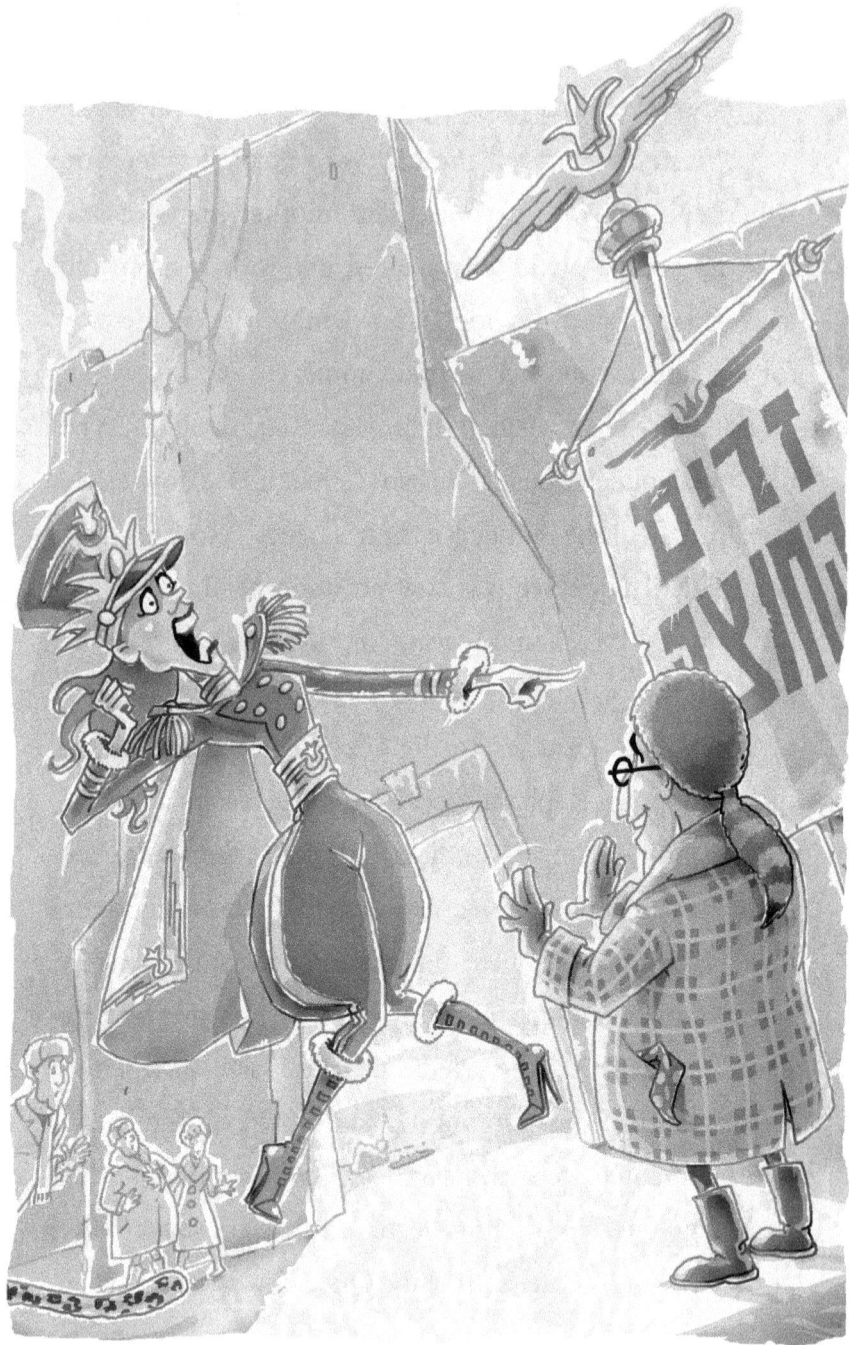

frightened? After all, you issued this decree yourself!"

"'I did?'"

"'Yes, you, Queen Decrioly the One and Only, decreed this.'"

"'Here? In *this* city?'"

"'Of course, this is the city you reign over—Decria.'"

"'Decria!' asked the queen in surprise. "I am in Decria? You are citizens of Decria?'"

"'Of course,' said the people.

'The queen began to calm down. Now she understood where she was. "How fortunate that I am in Decria. What a splendid city!" she said, and then she called out, "Hear ye, hear ye! I hereby issue a new decree!"

'*Oh dear*, I thought to myself, *she hasn't learned a thing*.

"'I decree to myself to be nice and not mean!" proclaimed the queen. "From today and forever more, I will not issue any more decrees! And if I violate this decree, I will have myself executed under an elephant's foot!"

'The people couldn't believe their ears. They all cheered for the queen, rejoiced, and made merry. And that is how they stopped suffering from the decrees of Queen Decrioly the One and Only,' said Uncle Leo, smiling at me.

'Lucky you dug in the right direction,' I told Uncle Leo, after a moment's thought.

'Yes,' said Uncle Leo. 'It really was lucky.'

That evening, before going to bed, I went to Graham's room to tell him about Decria and maybe invite him to a game of checkers. The sign saying 'No Strangers Allowed!' wasn't there any more, so I went in. But before I got a chance to say anything, Graham said, 'Get out of here!'

'Why?' I asked.

'Didn't you see the new sign?' said Graham. He went to the door and hung up a new sign. This one read: 'No Little Kids Allowed.'

'Who gets to say who a little kid is?' I asked.

'I do,' said Graham. 'Anyone smaller than me is a little kid.'

'But I'm only two centimeters shorter than you,' I told Graham. 'I'm almost your size!'

'That doesn't matter,' said Graham. 'Anyone who is little can't come in here. Get out right now!'

I had no choice. Checkerboard in hand, I left his room.

# Uncle Leo Meets the Real Uncle Leo

On the following Wednesday, I was standing in front of the bathroom mirror. I thought I was alone. Graham, Mom and Dad weren't around. I looked at my face and crinkled my nose. I bared my teeth. I made all sorts of faces at myself. A scary face, a funny face, a monster face. I was having so much fun that I didn't notice my brother Graham peeking into the bathroom. I heard giggling behind me and only then did I see Graham's reflection in the mirror. He was standing in the doorway and burst out laughing.

'You're crazy!' he said.

I was surprised to see my brother, but more than that,

I was embarrassed.

Graham ran through the house, yelling, 'Andy's crazy, Andy's crazy!'

My face in the mirror showed just how embarrassed and insulted I was. My brother had caught me red-handed. 'What happened?' I suddenly heard a voice outside the bathroom. 'What's all the shouting about?' Uncle Leo appeared at the door. 'What's going on, Andy?' he asked. 'Have you really gone crazy?'

'No,' I said. But I didn't tell Uncle Leo why Graham was making fun of me.

Uncle Leo looked at me and at the mirror. 'Making faces in front of the mirror, eh?' he said. 'I'm quite an expert at that. I can stand in front of the mirror for hours and make faces.'

'Really?' I said. 'You make faces at the mirror?'

'Sure do. Though once I found out that it can be scary.'

'Scary? Making faces in front of the mirror?'

'Well,' said Uncle Leo, narrowing his eyes. 'Not all mirrors are ordinary. Some mirrors are dangerous.'

'Dangerous mirrors? What could be dangerous about a mirror?'

'Come along and I'll tell you,' he said.

So we went to the balcony and sat down, and Uncle Leo started talking.

'Once, when I was visiting a bazaar on the outskirts of the Siberian jungle, I got up in the morning and went into the bathroom. I wanted to shave and comb my four hairs, and maybe even dye them yellow or purple. But when I looked above the sink, I noticed that there was no mirror. How could I see myself? How would I know whether to comb my four hairs to the right or to the left, to the front or to the back?

'I walked to the market to buy a mirror. I went from store to store. There were dozens of stores, but none of them sold mirrors. Eventually, I got tired of looking and sat down at a tea stall.

'"Why do you look so tired and scruffy?" asked the stall owner.

'"I don't have a mirror," I explained. "I can't comb my hair. I can't shave. I looked all over the market for a mirror, but couldn't find one. I'm tired of looking."

'"A mirror?" asked the owner. "You want a mirror?"

'"Yes," I said. "Very much."

'"There is a mirror store in the market," said the tea seller.

"'Really? Where is it?"

"'You see that big street over there?" asked the tea seller. "Turn right at the first corner, then left on to a smaller street. Then turn right on to a slightly smaller street. Keep going and turn left on to a very small street. Then right on to a really small street. From that street, turn left into a tiny alley. And from the tiny alley, turn right into the tiniest alley in the market. At the end of that alley is the mirror store."

'I thanked the tea seller, paid him, and set out.

'I walked and turned, and turned again, and turned again, and again and again, until I reached the tiniest alley. It was so narrow that my shoulders rubbed against the walls on either side. The alley was very dark, and there were no doors on either side of it. I kept going into the darkness until I bumped into something. *What's that,* I wondered. When my eyes got used to the dark, I saw a wooden door in front of me, with a small sign saying:

Madame Alleycat

'*What is this? Where am I*, I wondered. *This doesn't look like a mirror store! This doesn't look like any kind of a store!* I was about to turn around and go back to the big market streets, but all at once, I noticed something else written under the little sign:

Madame Alleycat

Mirrors

'*Hmm…I guess I've come to the right place after all*, I thought. I knocked on the door and waited.

'Nothing happened.

'I knocked a second time, and again—nothing.

'I knocked a third time, and this time, I heard rustling on the other side of the door. There was someone there. The rustling got louder, and then I heard the lock turn. The door opened with a long creaking sound.'

Uncle Leo frowned as if he had smelled something rotten.

'What did you see on the other side of the door?' I asked.

'On the other side of the door,' said Uncle Leo, 'I saw a woman with puffy, tangled hair. It looked like she hadn't brushed it for quite a few years. Her hair had all kinds of things stuck in it—stones, a key, a bottle opener, a banana peel, broken eyeglasses, a cherry blossom branch and even a bird's nest with baby birds chirping softly in it. But it wasn't just her hair that was wild. Her clothes were a mess, too. It looked like they hadn't been washed in ages. She wore a tattered skirt with a torn hem, a dirty shirt filled with holes, and a coat that was quadruple her size.

'"Excuse me," I said. "I think I have the wrong address.

I thought this was a mirror store."

"'You weren't wrong," said Madame Alleycat.

"'*This* is a mirror store?" I asked, surprised.

"'Yes," she replied. "Didn't you read the sign?"

"'Where are the mirrors?" I asked.

"'Follow me," said Madame Alleycat, entering the room with a slight limp. I went in after her. The room was empty. "The mirrors are in the other room," said Madame Alleycat. I followed her into the other room, thinking to myself, *How can such a dirty-looking woman sell mirrors? It seems like she's never even looked at one!* But in the other room, I found countless mirrors—large mirrors and small mirrors, wall mirrors and hand mirrors, oval mirrors and square mirrors, framed mirrors and mirrors with decorated edges—mirrors in all shapes and sizes.

"'You may pick out a mirror for yourself," said the woman.

'I went up to the first mirror I saw. It was a very large mirror. I looked in it and was shocked. I couldn't believe my eyes. I looked teensy in that mirror. Positively minuscule. *This is not a good mirror*, I thought.

'I moved to the next mirror. It was a little one. I looked in it and was shocked once more. In this mirror,

I looked enormous, gargantuan, much bigger than I actually am.

'I went up to a third mirror. In that one, I looked fat. My stomach looked gigantic, and my cheeks looked swollen.

'In the fourth mirror, I looked ridiculously thin, like a string bean. That mirror was no good, either.

'In the next mirror, my ears looked massive.

'In the mirror after that, my nose looked as long as a broomstick.

'In the following mirror, I appeared green.

'I kept on going, peering into one mirror after another, but was disappointed to discover that every single mirror in Madame Alleycat's store distorted my reflection.

"'All the mirrors here are distorting," I told Madame Alleycat. "In every mirror, my reflection is completely different from what I

really look like. I need a mirror that reflects me exactly as I am. Do you have a mirror like that?"

"'I have just one more mirror," said Madame Alleycat. "Try it. Maybe it will be right for you."

"'Where is it?" I asked.

"'Do you see the big closet at the end of the room? The mirror is behind it."

'I went to the closet, peeked behind it, and found a mirror hiding there. I took it out and looked into it, but couldn't see anything,' said Uncle Leo and fell silent.

'Why didn't you see anything?' I asked.

'I didn't see anything because the mirror was covered with dust. I wiped off the dust with my handkerchief and looked into the mirror again. Oh-ho! I was so pleased. In this mirror, I looked marvellous. Exactly what I really look like.'

"'This is a great mirror, Madame Alleycat," I said. "I'll take it. How much do you want for it?" I asked.

"'That mirror is not for sale," said Madame Alleycat.

"'I'm willing to pay," I told her.

"'That mirror is not for sale," she repeated.

'I took out some coins and offered them to her.

"'It's not for sale," she said again.

'I took out some bills and offered them to her.

"It's *not* for sale," she insisted.

"How much do you want for it?" I asked.

"Don't you hear what I'm saying? It's NOT for sale! Don't you understand?" said Madame Alleycat, clearly irritated.

"Madame Alleycat," I said. "I'll pay you whatever you want for this mirror."

"It's not for sale. It's free. You can just take it. Don't pay me anything," explained Madame Alleycat.

"Thank you," I said happily. "Thank you for the mirror."

"You're welcome," she said, smiling at me. "I hope you enjoy it."

'I left Madame Alleycat's store and walked back through the dark, narrow alleyways and streets until I got back to my room,' said Uncle Leo.

'But Uncle Leo,' I said. 'You told me that some mirrors are dangerous. It sounds like that mirror was a just regular one. Not dangerous at all.'

'That's what I thought, too, but it turned out that it was not a regular mirror after all,' said Uncle Leo. 'I hung the mirror above the bathroom sink and set about shaving.

I lathered my face and, of course, the reflection in the mirror did exactly what I did. I started shaving and the reflection in the mirror did exactly what I did—just like a regular mirror. Also, when I combed two of my hairs to the right and the other two hairs to the left, the reflection in the mirror mimicked me exactly.

'After I finished shaving and combing my hair, I looked at my reflection in the mirror with satisfaction. I smiled to myself, I raised my eyebrows, I opened my mouth wide. I started making faces at myself in the mirror. At first I made serious faces, then scary faces, then funny ones. After that, I held my mouth open with my fingers and stuck out my tongue. But then something unexpected happened that scared me out of my wits. The Uncle Leo in the mirror stopped making the same face as me. He just stared at me with an angry look. I looked at him in wonder, but he didn't move. He just kept glaring at me.

'"What nerve! What gall!" cried the Uncle Leo in the mirror. "What do you think you're doing?"

'"Me?" I said. "I'm just making faces."

'"When I was shaving, everything was just fine," said the Uncle Leo in the mirror. "Your movements were perfect. When I was combing two hairs to the left and

two hairs to the right, all was just as it should be. But making faces? I don't make those kinds of faces! Do I look like a clown to you? A jester?"

"'What do you mean?' I asked in confusion. "You're my reflection. You're supposed to do exactly what I do."

"'I'm supposed to do what *you* do?' shouted the Uncle Leo in the mirror. His face was turning red with rage. "You're the one who's supposed to do what *I* do. The faces you're making amount to mutiny. They're a disgrace! They're mirror crimes!"

"'But you are my reflection!' I tried to explain. "I am the real Uncle Leo, and you are my reflection in the mirror."

"'What are you talking about? It's the other way round! I'm calling you to order! Start behaving yourself. Do exactly as I do! *I* am the real Uncle Leo!"

'I didn't know what to do. I thought to myself, *This Uncle Leo in the mirror looks exactly like me. How do I know he isn't the real Uncle Leo?*

'I decided to ask him some questions.

"'If you're the real Uncle Leo,' I said, 'then tell me—do you like stories or hate them?"

"'Hate them.'

'*Impossible,* I thought. *Since I love them*!

"'Do you like adventures?"

"'No."

"'Do you like mountains? Valleys? Lakes?"

"'No, no, no."

"'Do you love children?"

"'No, I hate children! All they do is create noise!"

"'So what do you like?"

"'Me? I love to hate. Hating is wonderful," said the Uncle Leo in the mirror, sticking his nose up in the air.

"'But *I* am Uncle Leo," I said, "and I love stories, adventures, mountains, valleys and lakes. And I love rivers, birds and trees, too. And of course I love children."

"'Nonsense!" cried the Uncle Leo in the mirror. "The real Uncle Leo hates all those things! Especially children!"

'I didn't know what to do. I had doubts! I had fears! Perhaps the Uncle Leo in the mirror *was* the real Uncle Leo! He sure looked real. Maybe the real Uncle Leo hated stories and adventures, despised mountains, valleys, lakes, rivers and birds, and loathed children as well. Was it possible that I was not the real Uncle Leo?' Uncle Leo fell silent on the balcony, looking down and shaking his head from side to side.

'But Uncle Leo,' I said. 'I know you. You're real and I know you love all those things.'

'You know me, Andy,' said Uncle Leo. 'But when I was standing there facing the Uncle Leo in the mirror, I didn't know myself! I didn't know who was who! I didn't know who was real! I didn't know what to do!'

'The Uncle Leo in the mirror started yelling at me, repeating that I must do exactly what he did because I was his reflection.

'I was so frightened! I grabbed a towel, threw it over the mirror, and ran out of the bathroom.'

'And the Uncle Leo in the mirror disappeared?' I asked.

'Nope. Not in the slightest. When I ate, he frowned at me from the spoon. When I walked down the street, he watched me from the display windows of stores. When I looked into people's eyes, that Uncle Leo stared back at me from their pupils. The Uncle Leo in the mirror haunted me all day long! I didn't know what to do. I escaped to my bed, but couldn't sleep all night. I kept trying to think of a solution. Fortunately, towards morning, an idea came to me.

'When I got up in the morning, I went to the mirror and pulled off the towel. The Uncle Leo in the mirror

was standing there, razor in hand and ready to shave. He started lathering his face, but I didn't move. He started shaving, but I didn't budge. The Uncle Leo in the mirror got madder and madder. "Do what I'm doing!" he said. But I didn't blink. When he got angry, I began laughing. When he got upset, I laughed even harder. When he was

boiling mad, I almost burst my sides laughing.

"'That's the final straw!' cried the Uncle Leo in the mirror. He left the mirror and came back a moment later with a hammer in his hand. He swung the hammer and smashed the mirror. I jumped away, but the mirror shattered into a million little pieces. The pieces scattered all over the sink and then vanished, as if they had never even existed,' Uncle Leo finished his story and sighed with relief.

'And did you ever see him again?' I asked.

'On rare occasions,' said Uncle Leo. 'Sometimes, I see him staring at me from puddles, but I've learned to live with that. He might be real, but I'm real too.'

At dinner that night I looked at my reflection on the spoon. The Andy in the spoon gave me a smile, and I smiled back at him.

'Why are you smiling?' asked Graham.

'I'm checking to see if the Andy in the spoon is the real Andy,' I explained.

'What's that supposed to mean?' asked Graham.

'Some mirrors are dangerous,' I told him.

'Mirrors?' Graham asked. 'Dangerous?'

'Yes, in some mirrors you can meet a dangerous reflection and you can't be sure if it's real. Uncle Leo told me about it,' I said.

'Huh?' said Graham. 'Are you a little kid? It's just your reflection. I, the real Graham, am telling you that that's a load of chopped baloney.'

Graham might have laughed at me, but I just smiled again at the Andy in the spoon, and started eating my dinner.

# Uncle Leo Cries in Lafterovnik

I was running and stubbed my little toe on the coffee table in the living room. It hurt really badly. Just a second before, I had been happily running and skipping around, but after it happened, it hurt so much that my eyes teared up. I didn't mean to cry, but I did.

My brother Graham came in the living room right then. 'What's up with you?' he asked.

'I stubbed my toe,' I said. I tried to stop crying but the tears didn't cooperate.

'Why are you crying like a baby?' said Graham. 'You got a little boo-boo, so what?'

I had no answer for him. I tried to stop, but Graham's

words just pushed the tears out more. I left the living room right as Uncle Leo walked in.

I splashed water on my face, washed my foot, and then sat down with Uncle Leo on the balcony.

'It's not bad to cry,' said Uncle Leo. 'Except in Lafterovnik.'

'What's Lafterovnik?' I asked Uncle Leo.

'The village of Lafterovnik, in the Siberian jungle. Once, I almost got thrown into a pit because I cried there.'

'Because you *cried*?'

'Yes.'

'Why?' I asked. So Uncle Leo told me:

'I arrived in the village of Lafterovnik by chance, on one of my journeys in the Siberian jungle. At first, I didn't notice anything strange about the village, but when I went to the local circus, I found out that the people of Lafterovnik were quite bizarre. The circus was wonderful! There were clowns and acrobats in the ring, and they did all sorts of hilarious things. I laughed with all my heart, but I noticed that the people around me weren't laughing like I was. In fact, they weren't laughing at all!'

'What were they doing?' I asked.

'They were crying.'

'Crying?'

'Sobbing,' said Uncle Leo. 'The funnier the circus was, the harder they cried. Tears streamed down their faces and soaked their shirts. I looked around and couldn't understand why everyone was crying. After all, the show was very funny. There was nothing sad about it. A lady sitting next to me looked at me in surprise.

'"Why are you laughing?" she asked through her tears. "Is everything all right? Are you feeling sick? Is the show that bad?"

'"The show is amusing," I told her. "That's why I'm laughing."

'"Laughing?" she was surprised. "Laughing at an amusing show?"

'"Yes, I'm laughing because it's funny," I explained.

'"How strange," said the woman and let loose a wail when a clown entered the ring.'

'Why were the people crying?' I asked.

'That's exactly what I wanted to know,' said Uncle Leo. 'When I walked around the village, I found that the people of Lafterovnik were different from us: they laughed at the things we cried about and cried at the things we laughed at. When they heard something nice or amusing, they snivelled. When they heard a good joke, they broke down and cried.

'In Lafterovnik, hungry babies laughed until they're fed. When people got hit by something, they giggled quietly. On the other hand, when they heard or saw something that was really funny or that made them happy, they wept loudly. Sometimes they tried to hold back their laughter so people wouldn't think they were laughbabies.'

'And what did they do when someone tickled them?' I asked.

'They bawled their eyes out,' said Uncle Leo. 'Every time I heard something funny in Lafterovnik and I laughed, people around me got worried. They couldn't understand why I was laughing. They thought something bad had happened to me. I tried to explain that I laugh when something good or amusing happens and cry when something bad or painful happens. But the people of Lafterovnik just didn't understand.

'One day, they announced that the village headman's beloved crow had disappeared. The crow had lived with the village headman for many years, but a few days earlier, he had flown away and hadn't come back. Since everyone in the village loved the crow, they proclaimed it a Laughorial Day, which in Lafterovnik means a sad day.

'All the villagers gathered in the village square to hear what had happened. The village headman, Joyson Cryevski, gave a speech. I stood among the people. The village headman began by telling us how much he loved his crow, how faithful the crow had been, and how the crow had always squawked happily when he came home. "My Corvino loved his feathers so!" said Joyson Cryevski. "His shiny black feathers! On lonely winter nights, Corvino always slept in my bed. He was a true friend, and now he's gone. Vanished. He didn't come back home! I will miss his wings, his beak, his voice!"

'Everything the village headman said about Corvino was so sad. It really is hard to lose such a good friend. I felt the tears climbing up my throat and welling up in my eyes. I started sniffling as I listened to Joyson Cryevski's speech, and it soon became a full-blown wail,' said Uncle Leo, and I could see his eyes watering.

'But the people around me had a different reaction,' said Uncle Leo. 'They all heard their village headman's

sorrowful words and started laughing. At first, just a few were chuckling softly, letting loose a stifled giggle from time to time. But the longer the village headman went on with his mournful speech, the stronger the laughing became. At the end of the speech, all of the people of Lafterovnik burst into full-fledged, side-splitting laughter. After all, in Lafterovnik, they laugh at the things we cry about and cry at the things we laugh at.

'I, in contrast, just couldn't stop sobbing, because Joyson Cryevski's speech had made me very sad. Suddenly, a woman in the crowd noticed that I was crying.

'"You're crying?" she asked, staring at me with a smile on her face. "You're crying on such a sad day? You're crying so disrespectfully upon hearing the speech of our leader Joyson Cryevski? How rude!"

'A man standing nearby heard what she said and stared at me in amazement. "What's this? How can you cry on a day like this? It's immoral! It's dishonourable! It's an insult to our village of Lafterovnik!"

'The people nearby heard his words and stared at me.

'"Who is that? Who is crying on such a day?" asked someone else.

'"He's openly crying, as if there's nothing wrong with

that," said the woman next to me.

'"Who is this man? Who's insulting us like this?" asked voices from all directions.

'Joyson Cryevski heard the shouts from the crowd and stopped his speech. Everyone fell silent and looked at me. The village headman said, "What kind of disgrace is this? Crying because my favourite crow has disappeared? Whimpering on Lafterovnik's day of mourning? Blatantly wailing in our faces? Sobbing while we all stand here laughing? What scandalous disrespect! Did you think you could just cry at us all behind our backs?"

'I tried to explain. "Please listen, dear people of Lafterovnik, this is all a big misunderstanding. I am Uncle Leo, and where I come from, people laugh at funny things and actually cry at sad or painful things."

'A big, tall man standing next to me let out a short sob and said, "You think you can deceive us? Don't make me cry, okay?"

'I didn't know what to do. How could I convince the people of Lafterovnik that Joyson Cryevski's speech had really touched my heart and saddened me and that was what had made me cry? I wiped the tears from my eyes and started saying, "I'm so sorry..."

"'Sorry!" the village headman cut me off. "He's sorry. Not only does he cry, but he's also sorry! He thinks he can cry at just anything! Let him keep on with his crying in the tickle pit! Throw him in the pit!'"

Now, on the balcony, Uncle Leo took his handkerchief out of his pocket and blew his nose.

'What did you do, Uncle Leo?' I asked worriedly.

'I had no choice. As soon as I heard they wanted to throw me in the pit, I began running as fast as I could to escape. It wasn't easy. The people of Lafterovnik chased me. I sped through the village streets, and they almost caught me. But then I saw a tall cypress tree. I didn't know what else to do, so I ran over to it, and climbed up until I was clinging to its very top.

'The Lafterovniks stood at the foot of the tree and shouted, "Come down at once, you cheeky crier! Come and face the punishment you deserve, you rude sobber!" And I, I was really crying hard by that time—crying out of fear, crying from the insult, and crying because I didn't know what would become of me. The people of Lafterovnik saw me crying and were surprised. After all, they cry when something funny happens.

"'Look at him!" shouted a woman. "He's crying as if

this amuses him! As if he enjoys being chased! As if it's wonderful that we want to punish him!"

'Just then, the village headman reached the foot of the tree. He looked up and saw the tears pouring from my eyes. He heard the sobs coming from my mouth. He thought for a moment, then raised his hand, and all the villagers fell silent.

'"Pay attention and listen to me," said Joyson Cryevski. "This man is obviously insane. Someone who cries at such moments is a madman! He cannot tell the difference between good and bad! He cannot tell right from wrong! He's simply a lunatic!"

'The villagers nodded in agreement.

'"Such a madman is no threat to the public," explained Joyson. "What's the point of punishing him? In any case, he wouldn't learn a lesson from it. He will never understand the moral we're trying to teach him! So I ask you all to return to your homes, get on with your lives, and leave the poor wretch alone!"

'The people of Lafterovnik cast one last look up at me, and left. I remained there alone. When I saw that no one else was around, and that I was safe, I climbed down the tree and snuck out of the village of Lafterovnik.'

'That story was funny and also sad,' I said.

'True. It depends on whom you ask—me or the people of Lafterovnik,' said Uncle Leo with a smile.

The next day, as Graham, Dad and I were playing basketball, Graham tried to pass me the ball, but it landed on Dad's head instead.

'Ow!' yelled Dad, rubbing his head.

Graham looked at him and started laughing.

'What's so funny?' Dad asked. 'Why are you laughing? That hurt!'

'I wasn't laughing,' said Graham, trying hard not to laugh.

'It's like in Lafterovnik,' I said. 'He's actually crying!'

Dad and Graham looked at me, not understanding what I meant.

'In Lafterovnik, they laugh when we would cry and cry when we would laugh,' I explained. 'Graham is actually crying when he laughs.'

'Exactly!' agreed Graham. 'I was crying. I mean I was laughing, but really, I was crying.'

Dad sat down on a bench and said, 'Maybe it was a little bit funny.'

Graham looked at me with a smile, and I smiled back at him.

# Uncle Leo Goes Soup-sailing

On the following Wednesday, Graham came home from school and sat down on the balcony without saying a word. I came and plopped myself down next to him. I thought we could play some checkers. Graham gazed down at the street. I checked to see what he was looking at, but I couldn't see anything special.

At first I couldn't understand why it was so quiet on the balcony, but then I realized that both Graham and I were silent. Usually Graham is always laughing at me or imitating me or teasing me or refusing to play checkers with me. You probably think I was glad that he wasn't doing any of those things, but I wasn't, because I noticed how quietly he was sitting. That meant only one thing: he was unhappy. I looked at his eyes and they seemed to be red from crying. He just sat there, not talking.

'Are you all right?' I asked him.

Graham didn't say a word.

'Did something happen?' I asked.

'It's nothing,' said Graham but his eyes told me the exact opposite.

Then I noticed a red mark on Graham's arm.

'What happened to your arm?' I asked.

'I got into a fight.'

'With whom?'

'I don't know their names.'

'There was more than one? How many?'

'At least three. Big kids. Two grades older than me.'

'Three kids!'

'Pretty tall ones,' said Graham. 'They kicked us off the basketball court. My friends ran away as soon as they saw them. They left me there by myself.'

'What did you do?'

'What could I do?' Graham answered me with a question.

Like every Wednesday, Uncle Leo arrived. He came to the balcony and asked, 'How are you, boys?'

I could tell that Uncle Leo had also noticed the look on Graham's face.

'Fine,' said Graham.

I didn't say anything. I didn't want to tell him what had happened to Graham. Maybe Graham wanted to keep it a secret.

Uncle Leo sat down. 'Have I ever told you about the time I met the giant who couldn't stop crying?' he asked.

'A giant who couldn't stop crying?' asked Graham.

'Yes,' said Uncle Leo.

'No, you never told us about that,' I said.

'So I'll tell you now,' said Uncle Leo, and he began.

'Once when I was visiting the shores of the Siberian jungle, people told me about a really small island—a tiny island with one coconut palm at its centre. Legend had it that if you dug a metre and a half deep at the foot of the tree, on its western side, you would find a buried chest filled with a marvellous treasure. The problem was, no one knew where the island was or what treasure was in the chest. The last time the island had been seen was by the captain of a ship that had passed alongside it. The captain wanted to sail to the island, but there was a wild storm at sea and the wind blew the ship away from the

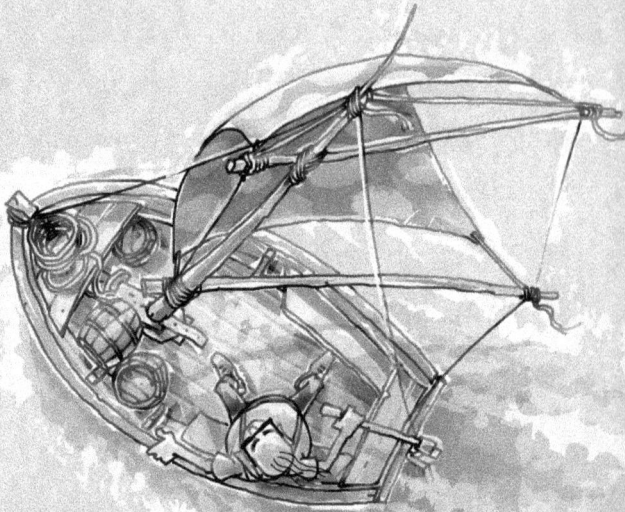

island. No one had seen the island since. No one knew how to reach it. No one knew what the treasure was.

'I wanted to set out to find the treasure, but everyone warned me, "No! Don't go! It's dangerous!"

'"What's dangerous?" I wanted to know.

'"The crybaby giant," they told me.

'"The crybaby giant? Who's that?" I asked.

'"No one has ever met him, but everyone who goes to sea hears him wailing."

'*That sounds like a make-believe fable to me*, I thought. *If no one has ever seen him, it must be a tall tale. I don't believe every story I hear.*

'I decided to go in search of the treasure. Even if I couldn't find the island, surely I would still have an interesting adventure. I took supplies with me for the way: a map, hiking boots, a canteen of water, a hat, a pickle and some bread in case I got hungry and, of course, a knife so I could split open the coconuts on the island and drink their milk.

'I sailed the sea in a small wooden boat with one sail and two oars. The first days passed happily by. The sea was calm, the wind blew in the right direction, and occasionally I really did hear long wails. *It must be the wind*, I told myself.

'I sailed on and on, but after a few days I ran out of both food and water. I didn't know what to do. No land was visible on the horizon. I was very hungry and thirsty. I was tired and weak. All I had left was a small dry heel of bread. I tried to drink seawater but, of course, it was too salty.

'*I wish I could catch fish from the sea*, I thought. But I didn't have a fishing pole and I didn't have a net. I didn't know what to do. Would I have to just sit in this boat until…? Until…? I didn't even want to finish that sentence. The sea was indifferent and the sun glared down ferociously on me. I looked around. There was nothing in sight except water. Suddenly I had an idea. I took my last piece of bread and broke it into tiny crumbs. I tied a crumb to each of my four hairs. That gave me four little fishing rods on my head. I bent over and dipped my four hairs into the water and waited,' said Uncle Leo.

'What were you waiting for?' I asked.

'For fish, of course. As soon as I felt one of my hairs being tugged, I lifted my head back into the boat. And, indeed, a small goldfish fell from my hair and fluttered at the bottom of the boat. It flopped around and jumped and turned and squirmed, and I looked at it with pity. I didn't want to eat it, but I was so very hungry!

'I took out my knife and prepared to cut the fish, when suddenly it began speaking. "Please don't eat me!" it said. "Don't eat me, please!"

'"But I'm hungry," I said. "I'll starve to death if I don't eat you. I'm so sorry."

'"If you put me back in the water," said the small goldfish, "I'll help you."

'"You'll help me? How can a little goldfish like you help me in this big sea?"

'"I'll do the best I can," said the fish.

'"Okay," I said, and threw the goldfish back into the sea.'

'What did the goldfish do?' asked Graham. 'Did it do magic?'

'Not at all. It just said, "Follow me," and began swimming. I rowed the boat with the last of my strength and followed the fish until we reached a tiny island with one lone coconut tree in the middle. I was so happy! I could drink the coconut milk and eat the sweet coconut flesh. I stepped on to the shore of the island and told the goldfish, "Thank you, you saved my life!"

'I climbed the tree, picked a coconut, poked a hole in it, drank from it, and then split it open and ate the flesh. After I had quenched my thirst and satisfied my appetite, I finally realized where I was: the lonely little island with a single coconut tree! I had found what I was looking for! If I dug at the foot of the tree on its western side, I would find a chest with treasure inside!'

'And did you really find the treasure?' asked Graham.

'I started digging right away,' said Uncle Leo, 'but I didn't get very far because all of a sudden I felt the ground under me shaking. The island rose up into the air. I was frightened and held on to the trunk of the coconut tree with all my might. *What is going on here,* I wondered.

'I looked around and saw that the island was sitting inside an enormous soup spoon. And who was holding the spoon? A giant was holding it, a giant who was more gigantic than any creature I had ever seen. A giant who was crying—colossal tears were streaming down his face. Every tear was bigger than a basketball! *It's the crybaby giant,* I thought to myself. "Oh my goodness!" I exclaimed. "The crybaby giant is real! He's not a myth! He's not a made-up story!"'

Uncle Leo took his handkerchief out of his pocket and wiped the sweat from his forehead.

'But what happened?' asked Graham. 'What did he do to you?'

Uncle Leo continued with his story. 'The crybaby giant had the island in his spoon. He opened his mouth wide and was about to swallow the island—and me along with it!

'"Hey! Wait! Don't swallow me!" I yelled.

'"Who's that? Who's talking to me from inside my soup?" the giant cried in astonishment.

'"It's me, Uncle Leo, here in your spoon," I said.

'The crybaby giant looked at the spoon and saw me for the first time.

"What are you doing on this dumpling?" he asked, weeping as he spoke. "What kind of fish are you?"

"'I'm not a fish," I tried to explain. "I'm a human being and I'm looking for treasure."

"'Treasure? In my fish soup?"

"'It's a pretty small treasure. A tiny treasure hidden on this island."

"'Island? This isn't an island. It's a dumpling in my soup!" bawled the giant. "I must eat the dumpling. This fish soup is too salty. The dumpling makes it sweet!" he yelled.

'I understood that the crybaby giant drank the sea like soup.

"'Why is your soup so salty?" I asked. "Perhaps I can help you."

"'You? Help *me*? How can a little creature like you help a big creature like me?"

"'I'll do the best I can," I said. "Tell me, why is this soup so salty?"

"'Because my salty tears are falling in it."

"'And why are you crying?" I asked.

"'Because the soup is salty. And it really doesn't taste good!" grumbled the giant.

'"You're crying because the soup is salty," I repeated, "and the soup is salty because you're crying?"

'The giant nodded his head and let out a long whimper.

'I tried to explain to the giant that there was no reason to cry. If he stopped crying, his tears would stop salting the soup. Eventually it would rain, and the soup would be sweeter.

'But the crybaby giant just kept crying. "It's too salty!" he wailed.

'I tried to explain again and again, but the giant wouldn't listen. He just kept on crying.

'"Stop it!" he screamed. "You're not helping at all. I'm going to eat this dumpling and that's that. It's sweet!" The giant moved the island, and me, towards his massive mouth.

'"Wait!" I shouted. "I'll tell you a story!"

'"A story?" asked the giant. The spoon stopped moving.

'"Yes, a story," I said. "Maybe it will help."

'And then I really did tell him a story,' said Uncle Leo. 'In fact, I told him several stories.'

'What stories did you tell him?' I asked.

'I told him about my adventures in the Siberian jungle. I told him about the village of Lafterovnik, where crying

and laughing were switched. I told him about the Kingdom of Decria, ruled by the cruel Queen Decrioly the One and Only. I also told him about the Uncle Leo in the mirror, who claimed to be the real Uncle Leo. The crybaby giant listened to all the stories. Slowly he stopped crying, his tears dried up, and he began giggling. The stories amused him.

"'I haven't laughed like this for a long time," said the giant. "Thank you, Uncle Leo. My tears have stopped. Soon it will rain, and the rainwater will sweeten my soup, so it won't be so salty. I didn't believe someone so small could help an enormous giant like me. Thank you!"

'I dug into the ground next to the tree and took out the treasure. Then the giant carried me in the huge soup spoon and set me down carefully on dry land. He put the island in his mouth, swallowed it with a big smile and waved goodbye.'

'Wait a minute,' said Graham. 'What was in the chest? What was the treasure?' He had forgotten all about his own tears.

'The chest?' said Uncle Leo. 'Well, there was a scroll inside.'

'A scroll?' Graham repeated.

'A secret scroll?' I asked. We were both surprised.

'Yes. I've kept it all this time.'

'Could you show it to us?'

'Certainly,' said Uncle Leo, and he pulled a scroll out of his pocket. It had strange, unfamiliar letters on it, probably in the language they speak in the Siberian jungle.

'I'll translate what it says for you,' said Uncle Leo, and read:

*Stories are words made into sweets,*
*That, just like cream cakes and various treats,*
*For grownups and kids are the yummiest eats.*
*Your skin will be saved, time after time,*
*By true stories, tall tales or even a rhyme.*
*But there's kind of a rule you should never let go:*
*The younger you grow, the better you know*
*'Cause the smaller you are, the less you are able*
*To miss out on stories, legends or fables.*
*Either funny or tragic or even spine-chilling,*
*They enter your heart with a flow or a trilling*
*And play there a song whose music is pleasant,*
*Giving your life the most wonderful present.*

Uncle Leo finished reading the scroll. It amused us very much, and Uncle Leo said we could keep it. We hung it on the balcony wall.

After Uncle Leo left, the two of us played checkers on the balcony until Mom came and called us for dinner.

'Wait a second,' said Graham. 'We're in the middle of a game.'

Dad came in and noticed the scroll hanging on the wall. 'What's that?' he asked.

'It's a secret scroll,' I said.

'From the Siberian jungle,' Graham added.

'The Siberian jungle?' asked Mom and Dad, puzzled.

'Uncle Leo travelled there,' Graham explained, 'and had lots of adventures.'

'Someday we'll all take a trip there,' I said.

'Gladly,' said Mom. 'But tonight Dad's made dumpling soup, so let's go eat.'

And we all went to the kitchen.

Uncle Leo continues to visit us every Wednesday and tell us his adventures from around the world. It's great fun.

And Graham and I? We still fight, but some days we are almost friends. Sometimes we even play checkers together.

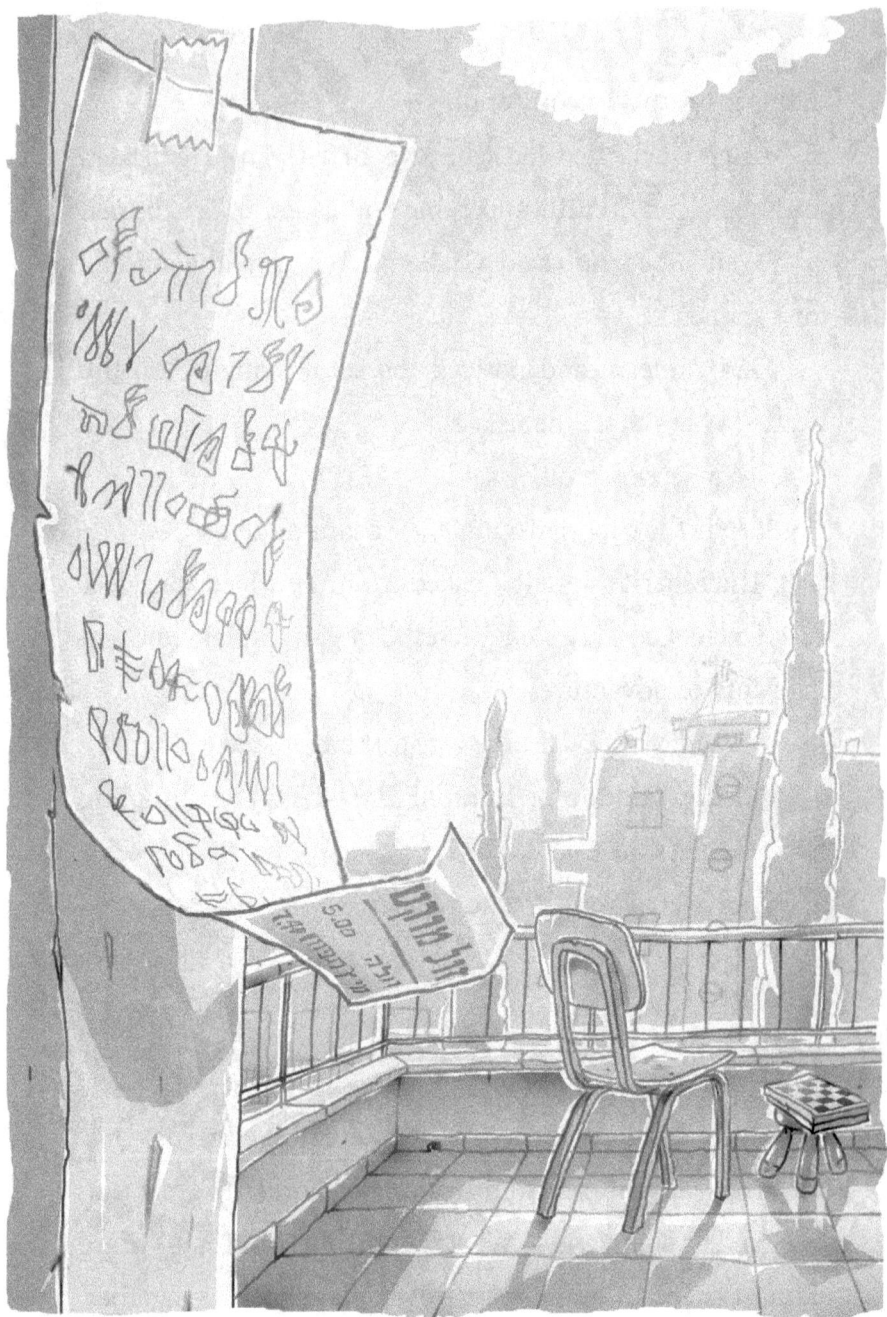